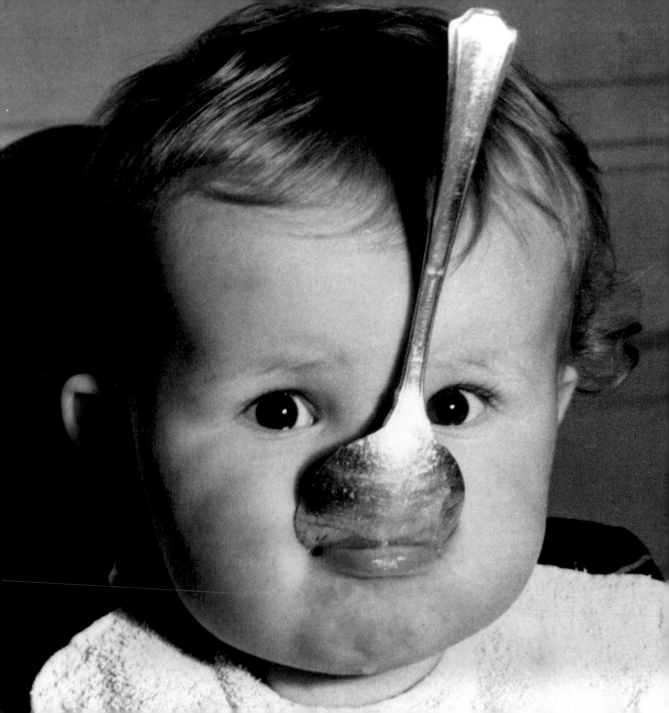

Funny Babies

EDITED BY
J. C. SUARÈS

TEXT BY
JANA MARTIN

PHOTO RESEARCH BY
KATRINA FRIED

WELCOME ENTERPRISES, INC.
NEW YORK

Published in 1998 by Welcome Enterprises, Inc.
588 Broadway, New York, NY 10012
(212) 343-9430 FAX: (212) 343-9434

Distributed in the U.S. by Stewart, Tabori & Chang, Inc.
a division of U.S. Media Holdings, Inc.
115 West 18th Street, New York, NY 10011
Distributed in Canada by General Publishing Co., Ltd.
30 Lesmill Road, Don Mills, Ontario, Canada M3B 2T6
Sold in Australia by Peribo Pty Ltd.
58 Beaumont Road, Mount Kuring-gai, NSW 2080, Australia
Distributed in all other territories by Grantham Book Services Ltd.
Isaac Newton Way, Alma Park Industrial Estate
Grantham, Lincolnshire, NG31 9SD England

The publishers gratefully acknowledge the permission of the
following to reprint the copyrighted material in this book:

Quote on page 22: "There Was a Little Girl," by Henry
Wadsworth Longfellow (nineteenth century).

Quote on page 38: "Keystones of Thought," by Austin O'Malley.

Quote on page 59: Copyright 1952 E.B. White renewed © 1980
by E.B. White Pennsylvania: 1974.

Quote on page 70: Groucho Marx™ licensed by Groucho Marx
Productions, Inc., represented by the Roger Richman Agency,
Inc., Beverly Hills, CA.

NOTICE: Every effort has been made to locate the copyright
owners of the material used in the book. Please let us know if an
error has been made, and we will make any necessary changes
in subsequent printings.

Library of Congress Card Catalog Number: 97-062338
ISBN 0-941807-14-2

Printed and bound in Italy
10 9 8 7 6 5 4 3 2 1

PAGE 1:

Erika Stone
MARLENA'S FIRST BIRTHDAY
New York City, 1988

PAGE 2:

S.H. Nelson
BUTCH WITH A SILVER SPOON
Rochester, New York, 1944

PAGE 7:

Erika Stone
MICHAEL AND HIS GERBIL
New York City, 1978

PAGE 11:

Erika Stone
SMELLING THE NICE FLOWER
Westchester, New York, 1979

The funniest baby I know is Jacob, who's thirteen months old. He has apple cheeks, merry green eyes and a cloud of strawberry blond hair. To put it in nonparental terms, he belongs to my close friends—their first and only child. He's their only child because, to put it in more parental terms, they belong to him.

Everyday is Jacob day. This requires his parents be as vigilant as if they're on a submarine watch, with a nervous, eagle eye constantly poised at that awkward contraption called parental foresight. But nonstop baby business is not funny by itself: if it were, nearly all parents would belly laugh entire days away, their laughter broken only by the Young One's short snatches of angel sleep. What makes Jacob funny is that he finds the whole world funny, and like a good comedian he infects his audience—he will *always* find an audience—with his merry light until they are laughing as hard as they can.

The Irish in both of Jacob's parents, in them diluted to just a twinkle in the eye, has resurfaced whole-hog in Jacob. His first two-legged step ever was a jig, danced for the baby-sitters at eleven months old. When Mom tried to get Jacob moving again, he refused. But when company came over, after staring at the strangers from his father's lap, he eased himself onto the floor, made sure they were watching, and tossed himself into a little dance. "Eeee!" he sang, and after checking their attention span (they were transfixed), he scrunched up his face and shifted his voice into a very unbabylike growl that sounded like Donald Duck on helium. "Yuh yuh!" he said, jigging around.

"My gosh!" his mother said. "They told me he could dance, but I didn't believe it."

The guests looked a little sideways at her, wondering who *they* were. Perhaps Mommy was a little tired?

acob wants to laugh like some kids want to eat. And he doesn't want to laugh alone. But he doesn't care if his parents laugh. It's bigger payback he's after. He's off like a shot down the living room, heading for the cat on the rug, and Grandma (visiting from across the country) is right behind him, trying to avert disaster. But Jacob's too fast. The cat skitters away *and* knocks over the beer on the coffee table, and Jacob screams with delight. It's so funny! All this crazy action and hysteria! Things will not stop tumbling and crashing in this cat's wake! Books go thump, a guitar goes clangggg, the phone rings as it hits the floor. This makes Jacob want to laugh. But is Grandma laughing? She's not. She's actually frowning and a bit out of breath. This darn mischievous little devil! she's thinking. So Jacob gives her that *look*. That studied, softly calculating look. He waits a beat, then begins to jig around the room, waving his arms. "Gahdeeee!" he sings, then stops cold. Checks her with his tremendous green eyes.

She cracks a smile.

Encouraged, he tosses a huge grin back and starts his circuit again, singing louder. Then he stops. Looks at Grandma.

Still smiling, but is she on the verge of—?

He takes his finger and starts to trip his lips up and down, just like Daddy showed him. Bubudubudubububuhdubah he goes, until he's really flying.

Bubudubudubuh—his eyes are still fastened on Grandma.

Grandma can't help it. He wants her to laugh! *She* wants to laugh. How can she stay mad? Her shoulders relax and start to shake, and laughter bubbles out. It feels good! And Jacob is delighted. He throws up his arms and claps and laughs too. Bubudubudubah he goes, loving this punch line so much he's going to repeat it till Grandma has tears in her eyes.

Tell me a story, I asked Jacob's parents, sure that they'd have a real bellyacher since their boy is such a card. "Okay," his father went, and then, silence.

"Can't think of anything," he said.

In the background was a rumble, a shriek, and more rumbling and shrieking, then a high-pitched, racing-motor sound.

"Jacob, no!" his father yelled, dropping the phone. He returned out of breath. "Rrroooo!" sounded Jacob, close by. His father had him on his lap to keep him out of trouble.

"What was he doing?"

"Vacuuming," said his daddy. "He had the curtains in the hose. Want to get down?" he said into the phone, though I knew he was talking to squirming Jacob. In a second came the sound of drums, relentlessly banging. Jacob's parents are musicians; their house has instruments everywhere.

"That you?" I asked.

"It's Jacob," his father said. "I told him you were on the phone, so he's playing the conga for you."

They never gave me a funny story, but I got fifty others from parents, doctors, day-care counselors, and, of course, my mother. "Don't do that," I whispered to her after she entertained my new boyfriend's parents with the story of how as a toddler I stuck the hose on our terrace through the fence, dousing everyone on the street nine stories below.

"Why not?" she said, an expression of complete wonder on her face.

"It's embarrassing."

"Well," she said. "You couldn't help what you were doing. You were just funny."

Then she thought about it. "At least I didn't tell it behind your back."

Cousin Jesse's mother did tell a story behind his back. Jesse, now in college studying physics, is a committed vegetarian. According to his mother, he's always loved animals. "As a toddler," she said, "he came running into the house calling, 'Mommy, Mommy come see my friend, it's a mouse it's a mouse, and it's my new friend!' He ran back outside and went to show me, joyfully swinging it by the tail. It was a dead squirrel. A *very* dead squirrel."

You might get lucky. Your mother might tell stories about your brother instead, and you can revel just for a second that the joke's on them. In our family recurs the tale about how my sister (then two) planted a chocolate-covered handprint on the the pants leg of Paul McCartney (then rock star) when he was wearing a white suit. At the time he was dating Linda Eastman, who lived in our building. He happened to hop into the elevator just as my sister finished merging with a Hershey bar. Full of chocolate energy, she was grabbing for anything she could. "He just—appeared," Mom explains. "And she just—reached."

Do babies know what they're doing? "Absolutely," said new mother Sue Simonez, "but maybe I've been under a strain."

"Why?" I asked her.

"Why have I been under a strain?"

"Why do you think they know what they're doing?"

As proof she started another elevator story. Babies can pack a wallop in tiny, enclosed spaces. "It was very crowded," she said. "My two-year-old, who has never participated in any kind of financial exchange in her life, suddenly looked up at me and said, very seriously, 'I'll pay you back.' Can you imagine, given all the news of parents doing outrageous things to children, what everyone in the elevator thought? A lady glared at me. She must have been wondering, what kind of payments does this awful woman extract from her child?"

I repeated my questions to anyone I thought might have an answer. Do babies know what they're doing? "Absolutely not," said a nanny. Then what makes them funny? A child psychologist reminded me that it's we who think they're funny: they, on the other hand, are utterly serious.

Such was the case with Willie, son of a pediatrician. He was just being creative one day is all.

"My son Willie is nonstop," said Dr. Krasnevitch, first name Ellen. ("First name *exhausted*," she corrected.) "Before he takes a nap is always a risky time. He gets his best ideas then. I might walk in as he's hurtling over the side of the crib onto the floor—where he'll just land and giggle (he thinks falling is fun). But this just happened: I heard him singing to himself when he should be sleeping, and I went in to settle him down. He was fine, actually. Terrific. He'd reached into his diaper and was wiping it all over the wall. "Look Mommy," he said, "Willie's painting!"

"It's about territory," offered one day-care counselor. "In their own territory, they have the freedom to be funny." I thought of my little cousin, who at eighteen months would walk into a room and flip her dress over her head, diaper-mooning strangers.

"Territory? Hah," said a veteran baby photographer. "It's about sunglasses. Who can't laugh at a baby in sunglasses?"

This same cousin, when her father put a pair of white sunglasses on her face for a cute picture, wailed in protest and threw them across the room. What is cute is not always funny. Funny is the baby that pulled W. C. Fields's nose. Funny is Lisa, obsessed, at one, with the crack under the bathroom door. Every time someone went to the bathroom, she'd dash over and drop down to her belly, trying to spy. "She was a scream at parties," recounts older sister Nancy Shaw.

"Once you have a baby," my mother once told me, as if only in retrospect did she feel safe enough to divulge this, "your world is turned upside down. Between your telling me to eat a mushroom so I'd grow smaller, and Nancy (my sister again) knocking over the Christmas tree, I hardly remembered my name."

So. Busy *is* funny, just not at the moment.

While Paul McCall, a California father, told me of his son Paul Junior's activities, behind him was the sound of a little boy (weight, fifteen pounds) obsessively emptying wooden blocks from a box and throwing them back in. Put through such paces, wooden blocks sound like a cattle stampede.

"He has become mobile," reported Paul senior, "and our life has gone

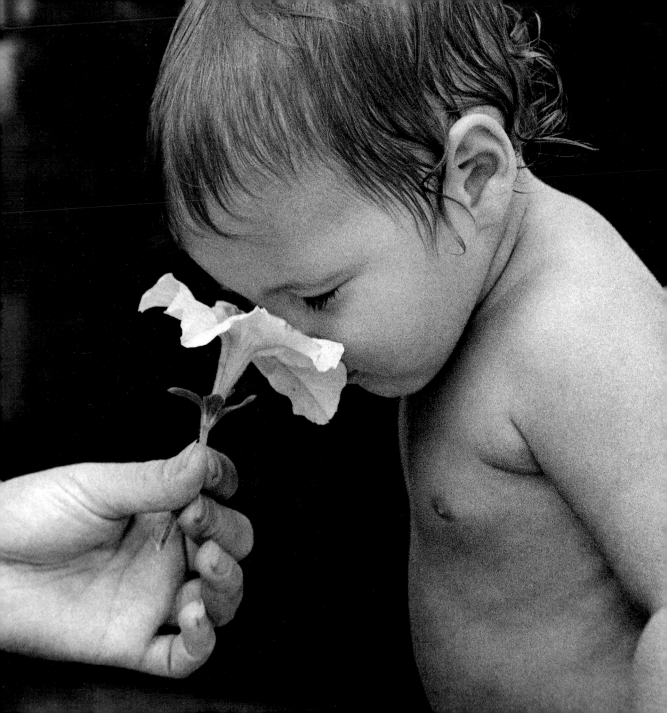

haywire. While his Mom works, I watch him. He's fixated on tin cans. They're shiny and big and heavy and make a big thunk when they hit the floor. So Paul empties all the cans out of the kitchen cabinets. And he's discovered paper, which is pretty and tears easily, and best of all, comes with the cans. So when all the cans are out on the floor, he methodically tears the label off each one, obliterating the identity of their contents. Then he watches me open can after can, looking for tuna fish and finding wax paste. He loves that, because it means we're having pizza for lunch."

That evening, Paul junior's mother called. "I just wanted you to know," she said in all earnestness, "that we do not feed our son pizza."

In the background I could hear that same cattle stampede. It was ten p.m.

"Is that Paul?" I asked.

"Maybe the next one will be a girl," she answered.

To Paul's parents, photographer Janicia Cannon offers the advice, "Wish for a boy." She has a two-year-old daughter named Ramie. And a sheepdog named Peach, "who's like a big floppy sweatshirt," she said. "He lets Ramie do anything she wants. She can ride him like a pony, or nap on his belly, and he'll just stay there stoically, hardly moving. Still, we've tried to teach her to respect that he's an animal—with teeth. One day I was doing the laundry and heard barking and shouting coming from Ramie's room. I dropped everything and ran, expecting the worst. But in fact it was so comical that I just stood in Ramie's doorway, laughing. Ramie had decided to play photographer, and had covered Peach in all her clean laundry— shirts, overalls, socks. She was trying to make Peach stand still. She had her big play camera with a big fake flash on it, and every time she pressed it—about twenty times a minute—Peach barked and Ramie yelled at him to stand still. Finally I interrupted her to give poor Peach a break, and Ramie said, "See Mommy? No problem with Doggie!"

"Babies *don't* know what they're doing," offered another expert, "but their personalities are so *novel* to us that we find them funny."

I mulled this over silently.

"You there?" he asked, a bit nasally.

"Seems complicated . . ." I began, and then gave up. If babies are funny, they just are. By virtue of their existence they're already scene-stealers: who can resist staring at one? Sometimes they just happen to turn the scene into a Three Stooges gag. As did the girl who quietly toddled over to her pediatrician—as he was trying to professionally convince her parents that her manic activities should be welcomed as growing curiosity—and smacked his toe so hard with a toy hammer that he screamed. Or Sandy Cohen's daughter, overheard talking to her doll: "Now Mommy's going to a meeting and will be back soon. So be good and don't sit on the antique chairs."

Humor, my father once told me, is always at someone's expense. But who can hold a grudge against a baby? As proof, one last story about mealtimes, left on my answering machine by Sammy's mother, and reprinted here verbatim.

"Hi, this is Claire Siversen. Sorry, but I can't think of a story. Here's why.

"This is my morning:

"'Sammy, open up and eat your strained peaches, mmm, good.'

"(Shriek, clatter of utensils and plate hitting the floor.)

"This is my afternoon:

"'Sammy, open up for your chicken, yum yum yum.'

"(Scream, clatter of utensils and plate hitting the floor.)

"This is evening:

"'Ooh Sammy, try the delicious peas!'

"(Shriek, scream, clatter of utensils, bottle of baby food and plates hitting the floor.)"

JANA MARTIN

Soap and education are not as

sudden as a massacre, but they

are more deadly in the long run.

MARK TWAIN

Ursula Markus
BALANCING WORK WITH A
FOURTEEN-MONTH-OLD GIRL
Zurich, 1995

Every survival kit should

include a sense of humor.

ANONYMOUS

Erika Stone
MY SON MICHAEL DOES A NO NO
New York City, 1976

Robin Schwartz
ROCKY AND ASHLEY
New York City, 1987

Karl Baden
HERE COMES TROUBLE
Plymouth, Massachusetts

RIGHT:

L. R. LeGrin
YOU DON'T SAY!
New York, c. 1960

There was a little girl

Who had a little curl

Right in the middle of her forehead;

And when she was good

She was very, very good,

But when she was bad she was horrid.

HENRY WADSWORTH LONGFELLOW

Karl Baden
FRIGHT WIG
Cambridge, Massachusetts, 1996

My son Rafi, who is a year and a half, has absolutely no sense of humor. He is very serious. "Rafi" I say, and make clown faces and stick out my tongue. He looks at me and runs his hand through his black hair and sighs deeply. "Hey, look at silly Mommy!" I say, as his mother does a crazy dance that even makes me laugh. Nothing. He furrows his brow like he's running equations in his little head. We got pretty worried until the day we realized what was up. He saves his emotions for the dog. When the dog comes around, Rafi's a different person. He makes lots of noises and waves his arms: "Dee! Dah! Deedah!" If we try to share in his glee, it just blows the whole thing. Rafi shuts down. Maybe he thinks we're ridiculous.

PAT CHUNDALU, FATHER AND SOFTWARE DEVELOPER

Harry Gruyaert
BABY WITH PHOTOGRAPH OF CHIMPS
Paris, 1987

OVERLEAF:

Express Newspapers
A PECK ON THE CHEEK
England, c. 1950

They're practically old men now, but when one of our kids was two years old, one early cold winter, he climbed into our bed. I suppose he wanted to get warm. And he said, "How come I can't sleep in your bed all the time?" So Jan, my wife, explained to him that only married people slept in the same bed, and then to get him off the subject, she said, "Well, who are you going to marry when you grow up?" And he said, "Well you Mommy, but we're going to have to get a much bigger bed."

STAN BERENSTAIN, FATHER
AND CHILDREN'S BOOK AUTHOR

International News Photos
DESNEE HAS THE LAST LAP
London, 1950

My niece Sonya is two now, and she likes to go with her mother to work. Her mother's a dentist. Sonya likes to sit in a little high chair next to the patient and play assistant. I got to see this when my mother decided to get some free dental work. Now Sonya ordinarily loves my mother more than anyone and acts like any cute two-year-old with Grandma. But this was not an ordinary day with Grandma. As soon as we got into the office, Sonya behaved completely differently. Grandma tried to cajole her into being cute, and Sonya would not have it. "Get in the chair, please," she said to Grandma, as Sonya's mother got out all her implements, and then Sonya climbed into the high chair. "Is this good?" Grandma said to Sonya, and Sonya said nothing. Then she very gently, very seriously put the waterdrain into Grandma's mouth. She had an incredibly impartial, almost distracted look on her face as she did it: she'd learned that cold, clinical look of a dental assistant who focuses only on the inside of people's mouths all day. Grandma fidgeted around and tried to tickle Sonya. Sonya folded her arms calmly and waited. Then Grandma tried to adjust the waterdrain to make it more comfortable, and Sonya deliberately adjusted it back. "Please be good," she said to Grandma, "and then we can all go home."

NINA MANKIN, AUNT AND PERFORMER

Dorien Leigh, Ltd.
BRUSH YOUR TEETH
England, c. 1950

FIRST WORDS

My friend is a new mom. She tells me about her baby, Sam, all the time. My favorite new development is that Sam, who is nine months old, is now talking. He has a vocabulary of about ten words that he uses constantly, but none of them are "Mama." Instead there's words like "Keekee" for kitty, "ba-bow" when he wants to be put in his bouncing swing, "na na na" for things he doesn't like, "Roe" for hello, "gokah" for going outside in the car, and "Meeee!" for himself.

EVELYN MCDONNELL, WRITER

Mimi Cotter
ONE-YEAR-OLD MATTHEW GILES
WITH CHILD PSYCHOLOGIST,
DR. LAWRENCE BALTER, ON HIS
NATIONAL CALL-IN SHOW, WABC
New York City, 1985

Harry Gruyaert
LAUGHING INFANT
France, 1992

RIGHT:

Harry Gruyaert
BABY TAKING A BATH IN THE SINK
Paris, 1990

Jessie, my neighbor's daughter, has a taste for slapstick. She loves to laugh! She'll take a spoonful of strained carrots and fling it into the wall and laugh hysterically. Put her in front of a mirror and she can spend hours making funny faces and then hooting with joy. She loves to do things and then laugh about them. Bathtime to her is like a Laurel and Hardy movie no one else is watching. The duck splashed the water! What a riot! The washcloth flew into Mommy's face! Hee hee! Her parents are very sweet, but they're not really slapstick types. Her mother is a professor of religion, and her father is a tax lawyer. Serious genes. Yet they have this baby who in behavior bears more of a resemblance to Henny Youngman. Sometimes even after she's gone to bed, you can hear her in her crib, having a good guffaw before sleep.

MARK CORELLI, PSYCHOLOGIST

Arnold Tolchin for International News Photos
UPSIDE DOWN
Chicago, 1950

When you are dealing with a child, keep all

your wits about you, and sit on the floor.

AUSTIN O'MALLEY

Mary Ellen Mark
BEAUTY CONTESTANT
CLINTON ALBRIGHT
California, 1992

And whatsoever you do, do it heartily.

COLOSSIANS 3:23

Karl Baden
**THESE SHOES ARE QUITE
COMFORTABLE, REALLY**
Cambridge, Massachusetts, 1996

UPI Telephoto
**KARI PARDINI TAKES IN THE
SPRING SUN ON THE LAWN**
Daly City, California, 1960

RIGHT:

Harvey Stein
EASTER PARADE
New York City, 1995

Karl Baden
BRAND NEW LEOPARDSKIN PILLBOX HAT
East Hampton, New York, 1994

We couldn't find a baby-sitter and we desperately wanted to go to the movies, so we took our daughter Shaniece. She'd always been so good—we raised her to be polite, and we never say bad words around her. But sometimes babies just call it like it is. The movie was a tender love story, the whole audience transfixed. We thought Shaniece was asleep. But she wasn't. Halfway through, during a very tension-filled romantic scene when the whole theater was so quiet you could hear a pin drop, Shaniece came to life. She broke into hearty laughter, like I've never seen her do before or since, and pointed at the two on-screen lovers about to kiss. "See?" she said loud enough for everyone to hear. "Like Mommy Daddy when they make boom-boom!" Five hundred people turned to look at us, every one of them roaring with laughter.

CAROL JACKSON, MOTHER AND TELEVISION PRODUCER

Martine Franck
MOTHER AND CHILD WITH SUNGLASSES
1993

If the greatest gift of all is life

then the second must be that no two are alike.

ANONYMOUS

Mary Ellen Mark
MR. ASIA, SAMMY AYOCHOC,
AND ACKHAYA CASEY
Baguio, Philippines, 1995

Mary Ellen Mark
CHILD ACTORS, TWINS DANIEL
AND JOSHUA SHALIKAR
New Jersey, 1991

RIGHT:

Mary Ellen Mark
YOUNG BOY WITH MICKEY MOUSE EARS
Lutu Village, Yunnan Province, China, 1985

OVERLEAF:

Karl Baden
BREAKFAST
Cambridge, Massachusetts, 1996

Hulton Deutsch
LITTLE JULIE MARTIN
SLEEPING IN HER HIGH CHAIR
U.S., 1930

RIGHT:

Erika Stone
ASLEEP IN THE BACKPACK
Paris, 1975

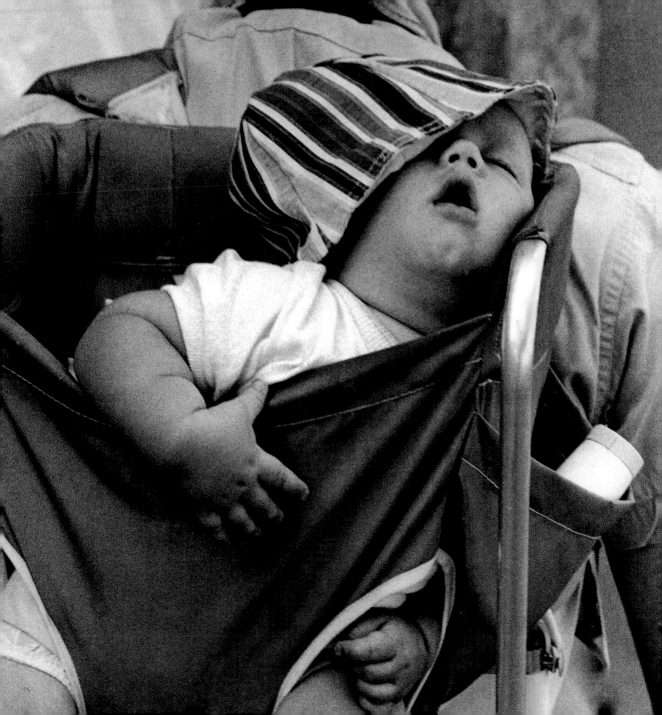

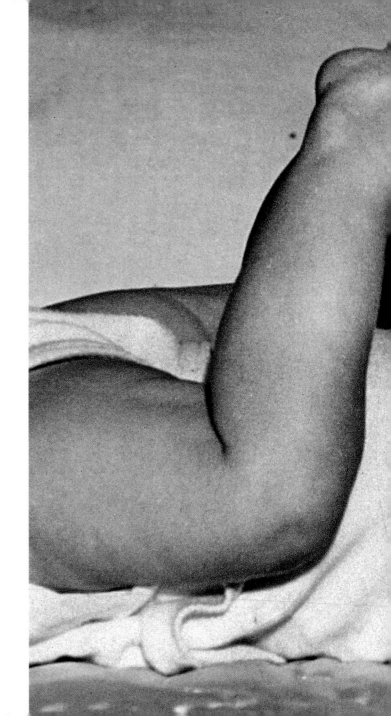

Popperfoto
LOOK MUM, NO HANDS!
n.d.

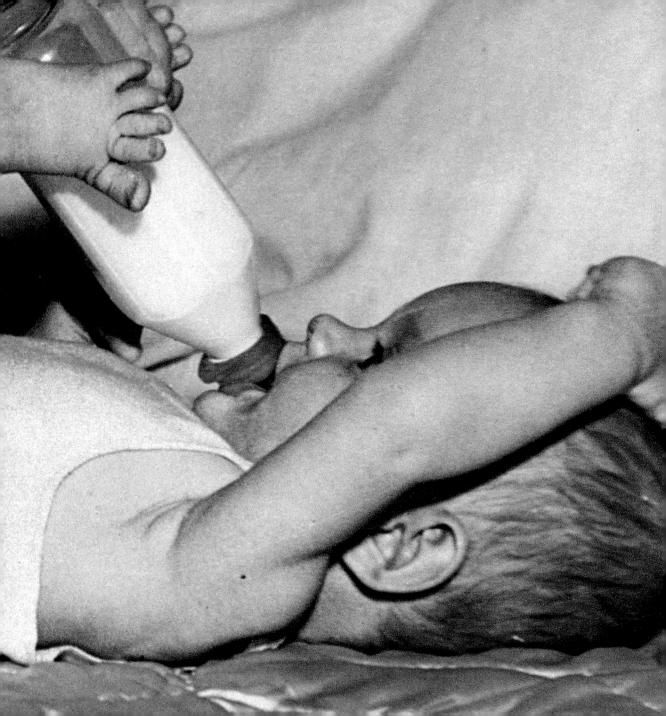

"What's miraculous about a spider's web,"

said Mrs. Arable. "I don't see why you say

a web is a miracle—it's just a web."

"Ever try to spin one?"

E. B. WHITE

Gregory Wakabayashi
WHERE TURTLE GO?
Georgian Bay, Ontario, 1997

Robin Schwartz
NATASHA AND ROCKY
Hoboken, New Jersey, 1993

RIGHT:

Dolores Lusitana
ISABEL'S LATEST TRICK
Prospect Park, Brooklyn, 1996

Babies are such a nice way to start people.

DON HEROLD

Karl Baden
WHATEVER YOU SAY
Cambridge, Massachusetts, 1994

David M. Grossman
**EIGHT MONTHS OLD AND
EXPRESSING ITSELF**
U.S., 1988

RIGHT:
Chris Steele-Perkins
CEDRIC IN TOO LARGE A POTTY
London, 1991

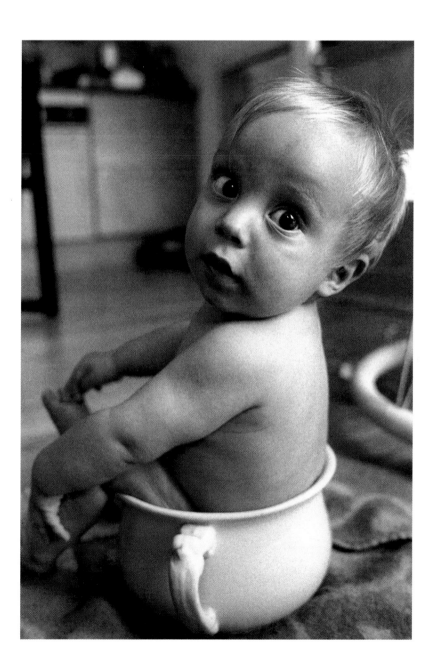

My daughter Nancy was what you'd call a busy baby. She was very strong, quick, and curious. So the house came under a state of siege. For instance, she enjoyed eating so much, she just wanted to eat anything she could. She ate the foam rubber pads underneath our rugs, and the paper jackets on our books. She'd just crawl around, looking for things to eat. For safety's sake, I'd put little chains and locks on all the kitchen cabinets. So every time I went into the kitchen and opened them, she could hear the chains tinkling, and she'd rush into the kitchen after me knowing that for a moment, forbidden territory would be at her reach.

MYRNA MARTIN, MOTHER AND ARTIST

Karl Baden
**I'M READY FOR MY
CLOSEUP, MR. DEMILLE**
Cambridge, Massachusetts, 1995

When our son was almost two, we took him with us to Legal Seafood—a great and not cheap fish restaurant in Boston. We were on a tight budget but we wanted to celebrate my birthday, and we figured that by now Neil was old enough to come too. It was his first time in a restaurant and we kept waiting for him to do something like throw food and have a tantrum, but he didn't. He was very dignified. When it came time to order, my husband and I ordered economical, sensible chowder and beers. Then the waiter, amused by our little son sitting straight up in his chair, asked Neil what he would like for dinner. None of us expected him to answer. But Neil did. "I would like lobster tails and black coffee," he said, to my complete shock.

LAURA FABER, MOTHER AND BANK MANAGER

Kire Godal
WITCH AND DRACULA, TWINS
Balboa Island, California, 1997

My mother loved children—

she would have given anything if I had been one.

GROUCHO MARX

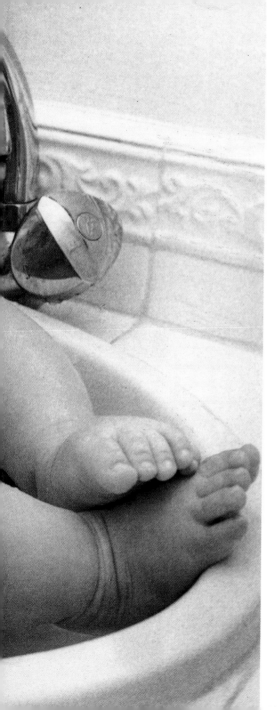

Karl Baden
**IN SYNC FOR '95
(NEW YEAR'S PICTURE)**
Cambridge, Massachusetts, 1994

It's not how far you fall,

but how high you bounce.

ANONYMOUS DAD

Richard Kalvar
INFANT IN A BABY JUMPER
1980

Harry Gruyaert

BABY IN A BACKPACK

Paris, 1987

RIGHT:

Richard Kalvar

**BABY IN A CAR-SHAPED RAFT
IN A SWIMMING POOL**

1997

The thing that impresses me about America

is the way parents obey their children.

THE DUKE OF WINDSOR

Harvey Stein
ON BROADWAY
New York City, 1979

PHOTO CREDITS

Cover, 21: L.R. LeGrin/Courtesy Archive Photos
Backcover, 1, 7, 11, 17, 55: © Erika Stone
2: © S.H. Nelson, Photo Researchers
15: © Ursula Markus, Photo Researchers
18–19, 60: © Robin Schwartz
20, 23, 40, 45, 52–53, 63, 67, 72–73: © Karl Baden
25, 34, 35, 76: Harry Gruyaert/Magnum Photos
26–27: Courtesy Archive Photos
29: UPI/Corbis-Bettmann
31: Mansell/Time Inc.
33: Mimi Cotter/Time Inc.
37: Arnold Tolchin/UPI/Corbis-Bettmann
39, 49, 50, 51: © Mary Ellen Mark
42: UPI/Corbis-Bettmann
42–43, 79: © Harvey Stein
47: Martine Franck/Magnum Photos
54: Hulton Deutsch/UPI/Corbis-Bettmann
56–57: Courtesy Archive Photos
58: © Gregory Wakabayashi
61: © Dolores Lusitana
64: © David M. Grossman, Photo Researchers
65: Chris Steele-Perkins/Magnum Photos
68: © Kire Godal
71: © Welcome Enterprises
75, 76–77: Richard Kalvar/Magnum Photos

Text: Jana Martin
Drawings: J.C. Suarès
Photo Research: Katrina Fried
Design: Tania Garcia